EVERYCHILD'S
EVERYDAY

EVERYCHILD'S EVERYDAY

Cindy Herbert
Susan Russell

The Learning About Learning Educational Foundation Series: 2

Anchor Books
DOUBLEDAY & COMPANY, INC., GARDEN CITY, NEW YORK, 1980

Anchor Press Edition: 1980

ISBN: 0-385-04155-1
Library of Congress Catalog Card Number: 79-7074

Copyright © 1980 Learning About Learning
All Rights Reserved
PRINTED IN THE UNITED STATES OF AMERICA

FIRST EDITION

ACKNOWLEDGMENTS

Many adults and children have contributed to the ideas of this book. Thank you, Cory Russell, Charles Hinojosa, Sonia Jimenez, Kelly Jarrell, Laura Jimenez, Bocio Briceno, Danny Hinojosa, Eddy Jimenez, Selva Briceno, Howie Miura, Cathy Liu, Meg Hathaway, Susie Monday, Weisie Clement, Julia Jarrell, Jearnine Wagner and Susan Russell. C.H.

FOREWORD

This is in fact a most unique and exciting presentation. Moving beyond the customary rhetoric associated with children, *Everychild's Everyday* illustrates ways in which creativity can be enhanced among all children.

This volume is the product of many years and hours of testing, validating, restructuring and working with children. The volume also reflects the combined wisdom, experience, and professional competence of numerous individuals who have been involved with the extraordinary school — Learning About Learning.

The uniqueness of *Everychild's Everyday* is found in the fact that authors provide numerous strategies and examples of how we can foster and encourage creativity.

More important, the authors make the point that creativity is a behavior and attitude, not to be restricted to only "bright" children or "talented" children. Rather, the position taken is that all children have creative potential and that each child is uniquely creative. Further, it is argued that creative behaviors are critical in every aspect of life — particularly in a constantly changing and increasingly complex society.

Certainly, what is presented here can make a significant and positive difference — if we adults are willing to devote just a small portion of our time and our own unique creative talents.

David Gottlieb
Dean, College of Social Sciences
University of Houston

EVERYCHILD'S
EVERYDAY

I want to participate
In the growing up
Of you
To know you're changing
Not just realize that
You've changed
I want to catch these
Moments
That will not come again
Tiny little moments
That are adding up to
You
The everyday
Of you
To catch the day
To find the time
To yield us
Possibilities
For being and becoming
We must design an everyday
That helps us to reflect
And redefine our
Every
Day
Our selves.

CREATIVITY INDIVIDUALITY EVERYDAY

This book discusses creativity and individuality in the context of everyday. It is assumed that creative behaviors are those most necessary in the present and future, that it is important to foster individual creativity and that the everyday living is both the arena for individual creativity and most critically needs the benefits of individual creativity!

All children have creative potential.
Each child is uniquely creative.

Creative behavior is necessary now and in the future.
Creative action benefits the individual <u>and</u> his society.

Creativity is fostered or dies in the context of the everyday.
Parents are vital to the location of creativity and development of creative action by their children.

If you at least believe this is true about your own child, this book will be of service to you.

When I was six or eight or ten
I knew what it meant
To have a lot of time that was
Really my own to fill.
Time was so invisible
That grown-ups never noticed it.
They were always saying
"In a little while" or
"Just a minute"
When it wasn't a very little while,
And a minute was time enough
To notice a lot of things.

And I really knew how to have FUN
All alone and even for free.
I knew how to surprise myself and
How to scare myself
And how to do a
Whole lot of things
There wasn't any way to say what it was
Except to say you were doing
"Nothing."

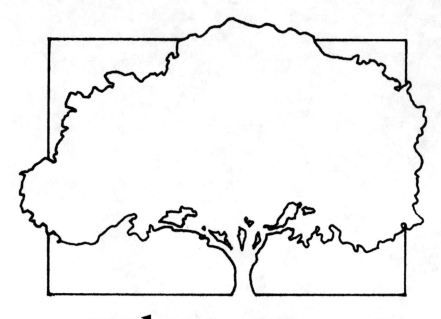

The Past

There was a time in the not so long ago when a child could be more like a child. Although children often had more daily responsibilities than they do now, their everyday was not so crowded and fast-paced. Hours could be spent in the intriguing business of getting to know oneself and one's world.

There was time to wonder, contemplate and daydream. Time to ask important questions and explore potential answers. Time to imagine fantastic possibilities and time to work to make them come true. Invention, experimentation and investigation were commonplace. Problems were more often seized upon with enthusiasm and confidence. There was time to have ideas and try them out to envision new identities and try them on and even time to make mistakes and try again. Curiosity was allowed a freer rein and led one onward to discovery. Learning was done for the sheer joy of feeling oneself grow.

Those of us who spent even a small part of childhood in this idyllic way know how valuable it can be. Those times sustain us as adults. It was in that way we came to know the best parts of ourselves — our strengths, our creativity, our individual uniquenesses. We still identify with many of the values, perceptions and perspectives from those times. Much of what we learned then, we continue to use to help us enrich, cope with and re-create our daily lives.

Did you ever —
— watch an ant struggle up a hill with a load?
— sit on the steps and stare?
— spend an afternoon in a tree?
— do a cartwheel 100 or more times till you did it right?
— make up scary stories to tell your brothers and sisters?
— build your own soapbox car?
— cook the whole family breakfast?
— find a dozen ways to play with an old tin can?
— draw design after design on the sidewalk?
— read under the covers after lights out?
— invent kitchen chemistry experiments?

We wish to preserve the best of the past — that part that allowed us to come to know ourselves and our own unique potential.

Now.
Now is all the time I'll ever have,
Or ever did,
Or ever will.
Now is the time
For the creation of now.

The Present

Today a child's life is crowded with sound and motion. Media floods a day with various messages and persuasions. Abundant goods and services tempt us from every direction. Comings and goings by car, foot, train, elevator and otherwise eat into moments spent at work and play. Time is more regimented with schedules, deadlines and appointments — even for children. Open-ended times are structured by toys, TV and relentlessly repetitive, predictable interactions. We are barraged by decisions, great and small, and the very richness of our modern opportunities overwhelms us with too many possibilities.

The everyday is too close to see clearly and too varied to analyze. We all stumble through the daily obstacle course, add our voices to the melee, puzzle sporadically over the meaning of it all, and sometimes turn off just for a quiet moment.

We no longer have silence and empty time and space unless we consciously make them happen.

Our present is a paradox. On the one hand, its diversity fragments and distracts us from understanding of our world and ourselves. On the other hand, the everyday provides rich, unnoticed, untapped and unimagined resources which could help us learn all we wish to know.

We believe it is important to plumb the potential of the present for its resources and relationships to the individual creativity of our children.

The Future

With things changing so fast, the future becomes harder and harder to visualize.

The tools children need for growing up are less apparent. Because we live longer lives, have more leisure time, gain more (and sometimes conflicting) information through the media, and in general have more opportunities and complexities in our everyday lives, we must be more far-sighted. In order to do this, we are finding that we must step back and reconsider many of the things that we have taken for granted: values, lifestyles, relationships, careers. All of us are having to become more reflective, analytical, and evaluative. We are beginning to see the need (and the challenge) to learn a variety of ways to approach problems, to think in new and different modes, to generate our own alternatives, and to change our situations to meet our needs. Flexibility, imagination, perseverance and creativity are the essential qualities we and our children must have. These qualities are the hallmarks of the creative person.

In the future, it will not be enough to be adaptive. We must also be creative.

We believe the development of individual creative potential is the best preparation for the future.

The Child

Creative potential is our unique human heritage. The ability to analyze and solve problems, to imagine and create, to explore new viewpoints, and to operate in different modes of thinking and behaving is basic to us all. We all have this creative potential — children, parents, teachers — everyone.

In addition, each individual has a unique creative potential, with a very personal style of thinking and working that is consistent over space, time and materials. This individual potential can flower most fully when operating with individualized and unique resources.

Real human growth demands the exercise of this creative potential.

Every child begins life with curiosity, the desire to learn and a unique potential for creative action. He has a special viewpoint and mode of operation unlike anyone else's.

We believe that the greatest contributions and satisfactions of the individual will spring from the exercise of his creative potential.

My everyday
Is my identity.
It is my now.
It is my moment
My new start
My chance to create
A new vision
For myself
For my child
What I make of this moment
Will determine
The story of us.

The Everyday

The needs, resources and actions of invention are intricately tied to the everyday real world. The everyday is the reality our children face now and in the future. If creation is the process they need most, then the everyday is the context in which that process must be exercised. The familiarity of everyday should not lead us to underestimate its challenge and importance.

First of all, the everyday needs are the most crucial ones: the need to improve the quality of our everyday environment, the need to communicate and work cooperatively with each other, the need to gain a positive sense of self, the need to make our work and play satisfying and stimulating, the need to create everyday lifestyles that are meaningful and fulfilling. Each of these important everyday needs must be filled, not all at once and for always, but through continuous and thoughtful creation.

In addition, the very resources for creative action are richly imbedded in the everyday. Each waking moment is an opportunity to create; each of the spaces and places in our environment is an arena for creation; each person, object and situation is a source of information for creation, each material and exchange, new or old, is a medium through which creation can be realized; our own thoughts, feelings, questions, and curiosities are the catalysts that lead to creation.

Finally, the patterns of everyday are the true legacy passed down from generation to generation. From everyday our children learn how to spend time, how to solve problems, how to interact with other people, how to get jobs done, how to see themselves and what to value. Our children learn interacting by experiencing, by repeated exposure to these same everyday patterns. What we do and say and where we devote time, attention and care will be best learned and repeated by our children.

We believe the constancy of everyday can either nourish or destroy individual creative behavior.

I learned it from you:
Not to wait
For the right situation
Or circumstances
Or resources
To find satisfaction
I learned it from you:
That my own actions
And attitudes
Can bring joy
That I don't have to wait
For the actions and attitudes
Of someone else
To change
I learned it from you:
That even in the worst of conditions
I can find one positive shred
From which to create a
Meaningful
Experience
I learned it from you.

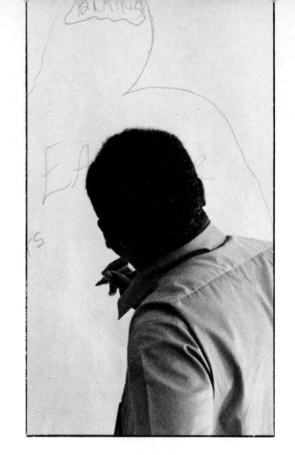

The Parent

Our children believe in what they see everyday. What we actually do everyday tells them what we parents think is important. Whatever we wish for our children will be transmitted through the medium of daily existence. Everyday, for better or worse, is all we have to give our children.

We parents cannot assume that the institutions to whom we have delegated authority over our children will really prepare them for an unknowable future and develop their creative potential. We parents must choose to prepare them ourselves. We may expect schools and other institutions to teach academic and social skills and feel that there is little more we can do. But, we cannot be sure that anywhere outside the home will our children have the opportunity to explore and develop their unique potentials. We alone are the greatest advocates for our children.

If we consistently re-think and invent meaningful everydays for our children, they will learn to re-think and invent as well. If we wish our children to be creative, we ourselves must be creative. The product of our creation must be an everyday — an everyday that allows our children to exercise their creativity, an everyday whose pattern expresses a creative process.

Our everyday should be an act of the imagination! Everyday must not merely "happen" but be designed to support the personal creative growth of our children and develop their potential for invention.

We believe that parents are the most important people in the location and development of individual creative potential.

Everyday is all we have to give our children

Goings and comings
Morning, noon and night
Seven days a week
Twelve months a year
Inside, outside
Front doors, back doors
Floors
Ceilings
Walls
Doors and windows
Streets and sidewalks
People, places, things
Family, friends
Feelings, thoughts
Big and small ideas

Waking, sleeping
Eating, cleaning
Travels and preparations
Work and play
Sound and silence
Rituals, rhythms, motives
Time and space
and
Energy
Perspectives
Plans
And messages
Conversation
Celebration
Beginnings, middles, ends

Everyday is all we have to give our children.

If I don't take time to step back
And evaluate my everyday
The shape of my life
I lose what's important
in the daily routine.

I forget what I need to remember

And the things I really want
My child to know
To care about
Go unsaid
Unseen
Unknown.

PART ONE:
CREATE

THE EVERYDAY

In order to help develop a child's creative potential, a parent must exercise his own creative potential.

The everyday can be re-created to complement the individuals who operate within it. No matter how set, limited or negative our daily lives are now, we still have a way of action — we can choose to make things better. Our children must know this. It is important that they see themselves as shapers, not victims of their everyday world. It is vital that they (and we) do not sit back and wait for the right circumstances, person, or occurrence to improve the quality of the everyday. We are the ones in control; we can choose to take charge or leave what happens to chance.

This half of the book can be approached in two ways:
(1) A parent can use it alone to practice creating an everyday for self and family. The parent's creative actions will thereby serve as a model to his/her child and family.
(2) A parent and child (or entire family) can try out things together and form a bond of joint creative endeavor.

The creative process is based on three basic kinds of actions. In this book these actions are called:

INVENTORY — find out what the everyday is really like and compare it to what you wish it to be.

IMAGINE — try out new ways of looking at everyday in order to generate new possibilities and ideas.

INVENT — put the best ideas into tangible forms, try them out in the reality of everyday, assess what happened and try again.

Each of these actions is necessary to the creation of an everyday — an everyday that in turn allows our children to develop their creative potential.

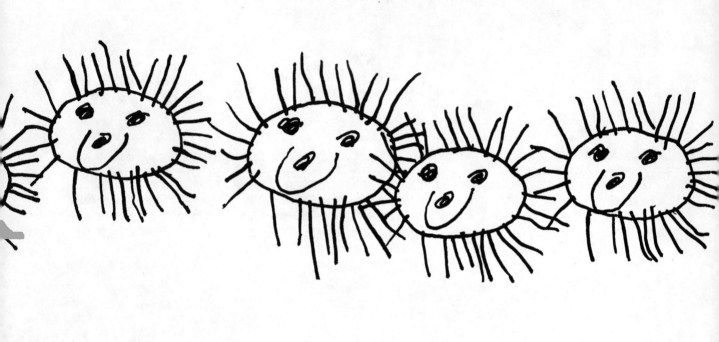

INVENTORY

Let me see
What's really there
Whatever it is
I want to see
Not just guess
By imagining
But know
From encountering
My child
My day
My reality.

INTRODUCTION

Creative action begins with the collection of ideas and information about everyday.

Everyday is so close it is invisible; so familiar, it is taken for granted. Our first job is to inventory the givens of everyday: times, spaces, objects, interactions, energies and feelings. We cannot assume we <u>know</u> the everyday but must find a way to tabulate what it is really like. In this way, we can gain the distance necessary to see the recurrent patterns in the everyday and their relationship to what we wish our everyday to reflect.

This section is one of the largest in the book, with lots of questions to consider and inventory forms to try.

We INVENTORY the everyday to find out what we wish to change, what we wish to keep and what we wish to emphasize.

Where is the emphasis every day?
What do we appear to be valuing?

If we really look at everyday, consistent patterns will emerge. Everyday rituals and routines will become evident as we see ourselves doing the same things over and over. A geography of everyday places will become visible, and we will see their relationship to everyday activities. Individuals and groups we interact with each day come into focus. Even the "things" of everydayness — the props, possessions and tangibles of life — will reflect our value in terms of the time and attention we give them. We will see the enormous role media play in our lives and how what we humans have shaped continuously shapes and reshapes us. We will notice the hammering insistence of everyday experience and the images of us it reflects. We will see that what we do, where we go, what we manipulate, whom we talk to and what we listen to; i.e., our everyday choices, create our everyday and our everyday identities.

16	**17**	**18**	**19**
23	**24**	**25**	**26**
30	**31**		

TIME

CONSIDER THESE QUESTIONS:

PARENT TIME

What times do I have? How are they always filled? What do mornings look like? afternoons? evenings? week-ends?

What times do I spend alone and what times with others? What proportion of my times are filled with what?

What kinds of recurring schedules and appointments do I have? What unstructured times do I have?

How much time do my duties and commitments take up? Duties and commitments to what or to whom?

How much time do I spend keeping the family going? How much time do I spend being chauffeur? doing chores? making rules? solving problems?

20	**21**	**22**
27	**28**	**29**

FAMILY TIME

What times does my family spend together as a group? What times are spent apart?

What times are structured for the family? What times unstructured? How do we usually fill unstructured times?

What are our favorite family times?

When do we work as a team?

What times are routine? What times are special times to be together as a family?

CHILD TIME

How much of my child's time is already structured?

What is my child's schedule of lessons, clubs, teams and other activities?

What time is not structured? How is that time usually filled?

How much time does my child spend all alone? What happens during this time?

How much time is spent with other people?

What happens during my time with my child? What do we do together? finish chores? talk? play?

SPACE

CONSIDER THESE QUESTIONS:

What are the spaces in my home inside and outside?
    rooms? closets? cabinets? tables?
    porches? balconies? patios? garages?
    windows? doors? walls? floors? ceilings?
    stairs? basements? roof tops?
    yards? trees?
    sidewalks? alleys? streets?
    neighboring apartments or houses?
What are the spaces and places in my community?
    stores? other businesses? eating places?
    schools? studios?
    churches? community centers?
    playgrounds? parks? gyms?
How is space used?
    for talking?
    for working?
    for playing?
    for resting?
    for studying?
    for hiding?
    for storing?
    for thinking?
    for enjoying?
How is space used by different groups? different individuals?
How do I use space every day?
What spaces are used the most by my family? What spaces are not used?
How and how much does my child use the spaces at home? away from home?

OBJECTS

CONSIDER THESE QUESTIONS:

What objects are attended, manipulated or otherwise used every day?
What objects fill my home and my life?
    furniture?
    toys?
    books? magazines? newspapers?
    clothes? linens?
    appliances? machines?
    tools? utensils? instruments?
    food? drugs? beauty products? cleaning products?
    TV? radio? other media?
    mementoes?
    art objects and decorations?
    junk?
    art supplies? building supplies?
How are these objects used?
How often are they used? Are they used too little — too much?
What kinds of purchases are made in a typical week?
What kinds of things do we throw away each week?
Which objects are used by the whole family?
Which objects are personal possessions?
How and with what objects does my child interact every day?

Family Interactions
    What do we do together?
        work?
        play?
        tease?
        fight?
        plan?

How do we talk to each other? What conversations do we have over
    and over again?
What do we usually talk about? What are consistent themes?
    each other?
    other people?
    money?
    ideas?
    memories?
    events?
    TV?
    health?
    food?
    rights and wrongs?

How do we continually interact, both positively and negatively?
What are our games — dialogues — jokes — private language?
How does each member function in the group? Who initiates?
    Who supports? Who keeps us going? Who makes final decisions?

INTERACTIONS

CONSIDER THESE QUESTIONS:

Parent Interactions
    With whom do I interact every day?
        children?
        relatives?
        friends?
        neighbors?
        co-workers?
        teachers?
        sales people?
        service people?
    How do we interact?
    How do I interact with my family?

Child Interactions
    Who does my child talk to?
    Who talks to my child?
    How often do I listen
    What does my child do with friends?
        family?
        teachers?
        classmates?
        me?
    How much do I know about my child's interactions?
    How many roles does she/he play in a day?
    How many functions does she/he have?
        student?
        babysitter?
        pet caretaker?
        joke teller?
        gang leader?
        diplomat?
        errand runner?

ENERGY

CONSIDER THESE QUESTIONS:

PARENT ENERGY
>How much energy do I expend in a day? Where are the peaks and
>>valleys?
>>mornings?
>>afternoons?
>>evenings?
>What do I find myself doing over and over again? What are the routines, rituals, and recurrent
>>emergencies? How much of myself do I give to each one?
>What kinds of pressures are always there? What kinds of rewards?
>How do I keep going every day?
>When do I give the most from myself?
>When can I hardly give anything?

FAMILY ENERGY
>Who contributes what to the family? Who sparks what? Who sustains us? maintains us? supports
>>us? renews us?
>Who sets the family pace? Who changes it? breaks it? matches it? enhances it? accelerates it?
>How do we get things done?
>>How do we get started?
>>How do we keep going?
>>How do we get finished?

CHILD ENERGY
>When is my child the most energetic? the most passive?
>To what does he give the most attention? care? commitment?
>To what does he give the least?
>When does my child give me an energy boost?
>When do I give him/her a boost?

FEELINGS

What are my everyday feelings?
  anger?
  joy?
  worry
  frustration
  irritation?
  loneliness?
Which are most typical of me? my child?
What events, situations and people do I associate with different kinds of feelings?
How long do I sustain bad feelings?
How many bad feelings does my child feel in a day? What circumstances summoned those bad
  feelings?
When do the people in my family have happy effects on each other? When do we respond unhappily
  to one another?
What do people in my family do every day to express their feelings?

WHAT ARE WE REALLY DOING EVERYDAY?

What is ruling our everyday lives?
What are we wasting?
What are we letting slip by?
What are we really giving our time,
    care and attention?
Are things the way we want them to be?

In order to create an everyday for our children and ourselves, we must decide what
    that everyday should be.

How can we create an everyday we really want?
What do we <u>really</u> need?

Do we need more unstructured time?

Or do we need to plan things more to be sure what
we want to happen happens?

Do we need more time together? More time alone?

Do we need to make use of more spaces? Or just to make
more flexible the spaces we do have?

What kinds of spaces do we really need?

Do our spaces allow us to work and play together and apart?
How could we modify them so they could?

Do we utilize the materials and other resources that we already have? Do we need to
look for even more? Which do we really need?

Do we need more energy as a group or as individuals?

Does our day need a steadier rhythm? Does it need more variety? What interactions do
we need the most? Which ones need to be changed?

Do we need to be able to have more ideas? invent more things to meet our needs? share
more? solve more problems? work more consistently? generate more everyday
satisfactions?

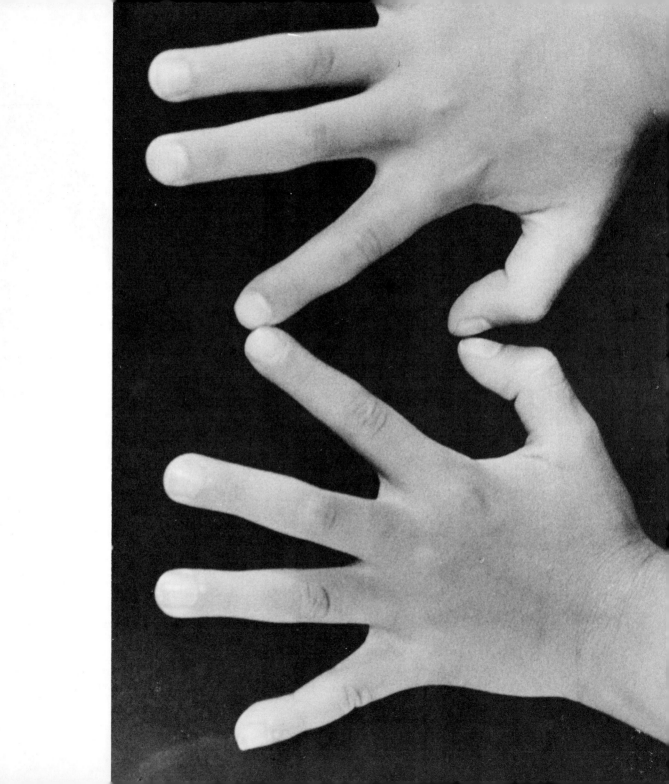

Without a few signposts
Sticking out of ongoing
Daily
Collage
I get lost
A few signposts to remind me
Who I am
Who you are
And why we like each other
What I want
What you want
And why we continue
Together.

INVENTORY
VALUES, HOPES, NEEDS

Inventorying everyday gives us a fuller and more realistic picture of what is there, but even to begin to create an everyday we must inventory further. We must enumerate present and future hopes, needs and values to remind ourselves what we believe should be the emphasis every day. Then when we compare what everyday is to what we wish it to be, we will discover what we must create every day.

VALUES

What is important to us? What do we cherish? love? believe? live by?
What values do we wish to preserve?
What do we wish to instill in our children?
To us, what are the proper attitudes toward life? work? love? other people?
What big ideas do we wish to perpetuate?

HOPES

What do we want from the future?
Where do we want to be?
Where do we want our families to be?
What are our expectations, dreams and wishes?
What do we hope will grow? change? remain the same?
What hopes do we have for our child?
How do we wish our child's life to be different or better than our own?

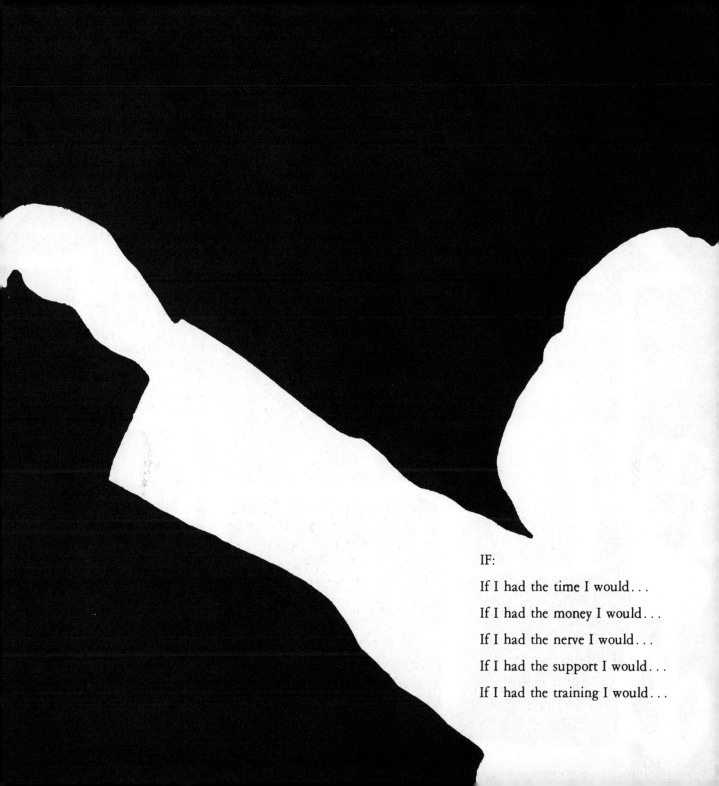

IF:

If I had the time I would...

If I had the money I would...

If I had the nerve I would...

If I had the support I would...

If I had the training I would...

NEEDS

What would make each of us happier? healthier? more involved? more satisfied? more fulfilled?
What really keeps us going?
What makes life meaningful to us?
What would help our family be mutually supportive?
What would help us enjoy each other more?
What would help us to grow as individuals and a family?
What, as we see it, are the most critical everyday problems?
What would make our home a place that nurtures and sustains our best qualities?
What would make our everyday a happy adventure into the ordinary?

MY IDEAL HOME

PEOPLE:

QUALITIES:

EVERYDAY ACTIVITIES:

IN ORDER TO GROW I BELIEVE FAMILIES NEED:

PROBLEMS TO OVERCOME :

Misunderstandings:

Depleting complications:

Old habits of dealing with each other:

Conflicting pictures of the way things

    ought to be:

COMPARE THE TWO INVENTORIES:

WHAT WE WANT OUR EVERYDAY TO BE
AND WHAT IT REALLY IS

Does our everyday reflect our true values? hopes? needs?
Are we doing anything to create a present and future that fits our values, hopes and needs?
How does what our everyday really is compare to what we wish it to be?
Do our children know what is important to us? Have we allowed our children to work
    with us to create a better everyday?

If we put our inventory of the everyday and our inventory of values, hopes and needs side
by side, we can begin to see more clearly where they do and do not match. These
comparisons will give us a place to begin to change our ideal everyday into our everyday
reality.

REAL

What I see in my everyday:

What I do in my everyday:

How my family interacts:

What my child now does:

Things I always say:

What I think is important:

IDEAL

What I wish it to be:

What I could be doing:

How I wish for my family to interact:

What I wish my child were doing:

Things I always do:

Where I actually spend the most time, money, effort:

How can I bridge the gap?

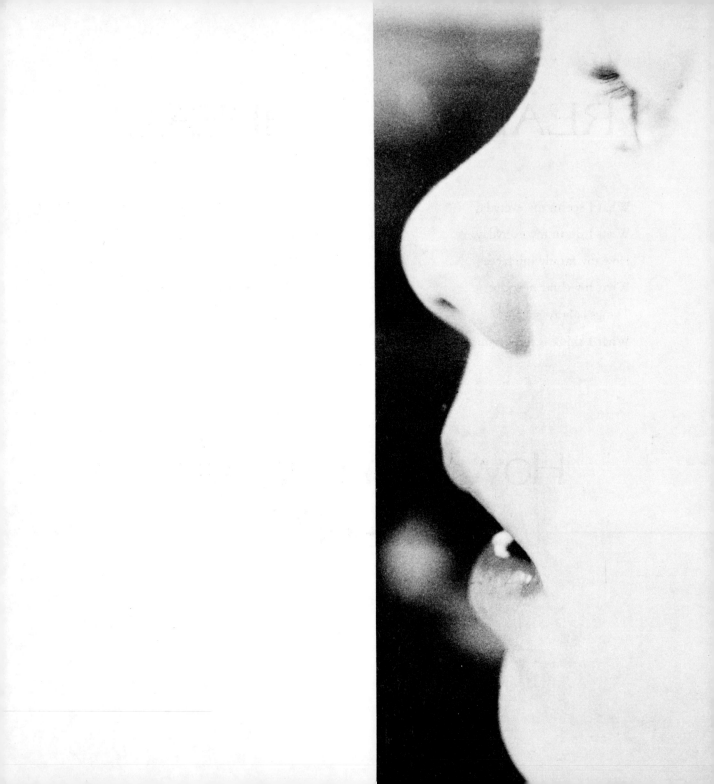

I need a time to think
And grow
To reach out
And feel the edges of my
Possibilities
Time alone
Time with you
Time to explore
What it means
To be
Me.

What do we

really want everyday?

(1) RESPONSIVENESS

We want to see our children staying responsive to what's going on, ready to put out energy, able to renew their own energy, able to change their habits, change their rhythm and make the best of each day.

If we see our children lost in bad feelings, we also want to see them inventing ways to change their mood and get going again. If we saw them spending large portions of the day turning off, we want to see them relearning how to be their own entertainment. If we saw them wallowing in boredom, we want to see them filled with ideas of what to do with time and pushing the limits of time to try out all their ideas.

(2) INITIATION

We want our children to take more responsibility for shaping their everyday. We want to see our children evaluating their own needs, making choices about how to meet those needs themselves and taking action on their own decisions.

If we saw our children riding through their everyday, letting what might happen, happen, we want to see them interested in taking more control of what's going on and arranging things to better support their own creative endeavors.

(3) DIVERSITY

Each individual has a unique viewpoint that we want him or her to be able to share with the others. We want the individuals to use their viewpoint to create forms of work and play in which the others can participate. We want each person to feel free (and perhaps even obligated) to initiate activities and directions within the family springing from their own personal interests.

(4) SHARING

We want our family members to enjoy each other — to be able to work together on mutual ideas, interests and inventive activities. We want to be able to share investigations, curiosities and creative productions. We want to do more positive and productive work together and take advantage of the power of group production.

(5) SUPPORT

We want to see our family members supporting the personal growth of the other family members.

As a family, we want each other to appreciate our differences, to celebrate our diversity. We want to promote those things in each other which lead to creative development.

(6) FLEXIBILITY

We want our children to be able to reflect on their own behaviors, let go of unproductive ones, adapt positively to new situations, learn new habits for working and operating, and practice new behaviors.

We want our children to be able to change old habits for new ones.

We want each family member to take on more functions within the family — to play more flexible roles.

(7) PROBLEM—SOLVING

If we saw our children grappling with everyday problems, we also want to see them generating dozens of solutions, trying them out and evaluating what works best for them. If we saw our child with only one way to relate to other people, we want to see him with many creative possibilities of how to contribute to a relationship. If we see our child in the midst of what is essentially a negative situation, we want to see him full of alternatives for modifying the situation, extricating himself or finding unexpected positives in it.

(8) RESOURCEFULNESS

We want to see our children make use of all that is available to them. If we saw our children not really using the time they did have, we want to see them inventing their own schedules in a conscious way. If we saw our children not taking advantage of the spaces and materials in the home, we want to see them with definite ideas of how to organize things to meet their needs.

(9) CREATIVITY

We want our children to act creatively no matter what the situation.

We want our children to see each experience as an opportunity to invent. We want to see them sensitive and responsive to their surroundings, able to pick up and generate ideas fluently, skilled at giving form to their ideas, and able to communicate those ideas to other people.

Whatever I am,
I am dynamic.
I am not static
Unless
I choose to be.
I also am not
Decided,
Fixed,
Finished
or
Settled
Unless
I
Choose
To be.

What could everyday be?

We wish to design an everyday to accommodate our most idyllic visions of our children and families. We want to create an everyday that responds to our deepest felt needs. We want to make a context for living where as much potential and human growth as possible can take place. To do so, we must hold onto larger visions and keep them in the forefront as we struggle to change and mold the more specific aspects of everyday.

WHAT TIMES MUST OCCUR EVERY DAY? WHEN CAN THEY FIT INTO A DAY?

Time to reflect alone for each individual? Time to work alone?
Time to share things with a child?
Time to invent together?

WHAT FUNCTIONS MUST SPACES HAVE TO PROMOTE GROWTH?

Spaces for quiet thoughts?
Spaces for sharing and discussion?
Spaces for experimenting? Exploring? Practicing? Inventing?
    Imagining?

WHAT THINGS DO WE REALLY NEED EVERY DAY?

Materials with which to invent, create, experiment?
Objects that please our senses and renew our spirits?
Props that make it easier to communicate and share?

WHAT INTERACTIONS DO WE NEED EVERY DAY?

Stimulating each other with new information? ideas? investigations?
Playing and imagining and trying out things together?
Asking each other questions to locate viewpoints, concerns, puzzles,
    problems?

WHAT ENERGIES DO WE NEED IN A DAY EVERY DAY?

Energy to listen to each other?
Energy to respond?
Energy to change behaviors — perhaps even on the spot?
Energy to maintain our daily needs?
Energy to get going? Keep going? Make transitions? Finish?

WHAT KINDS OF FEELINGS DO WE NEED EVERY DAY?

Good feelings about ourselves and what we're doing?
Feelings that we are mutually supporting one another?
Feelings of confidence that we and our children will keep growing?

We must carefully choose and reinforce those elements that will help us stay positive, active and healthy in the midst of the daily sameness.

In the middle
Of the movement
And the mind noise
And the muddle
If I see just past
My nose
I'm doing good
So I carved
A little time
A little space
A little silence
Just for us
So we can
Congregate and
Calibrate and
Cogitate and
Maybe even
Celebrate
Just what is happening
To us
Then return
To the motion
And the mundane
And the messes and minutiae
With a trace of a memory
Of why we're doing what we're going
Of how we hope to help things happen
And where our chance for change
And joy
And genuine exchange
Exists
In the middle
Of the maddening
And monotonous
   (but mostly
    man-made)
Meaningfulness.

IMAGINE

Join me in the serious work
Of play
In a gallop through
Imaginary possibilities.

Our first creative act was to inventory what is; our second creative act is to imagine what might be.

Essential to the creation of a new and better everyday is our own imagination. It is critical that we take the time to consider and generate multitudes of new ideas about everyday and what it might be. To do a good job, we must let off all the stops and suspend our critical selves. We must think big, push beyond obvious solutions and old answers and give our imagination full play.

Four Viewpoints

Here are four different ways to stimulate our imagination about everyday and generate new ideas:

1. **Starting All Over**
   Imagine there are no constraints or pressures upon us and that we can begin at the beginning to make things as we wish them to be.

2. **Wildmanning**
   Letting ourselves be completely flexible and imaginative to find new viewpoints for using what we have been given to work with.

3. **Getting Down to Basics**
   We survey all we have and ask ourselves is every single thing necessary. If we have to think twice about it, we imagine living happily without it.

4. **Changing Me**
   We visualize what we might do if nothing and no one will ever change but ourselves.

Use your imagination to create an everyday.

1. STARTING ALL OVER

One viewpoint we can use to generate ideas is momentarily to sweep aside the observations we have just made of what was in our everyday and begin at the beginning. If we had no schedules to meet, no traditions to guide us, no consensus about how things should be done, no routines to repeat, no pressures or responsibilities to handle, no chosen career, no possessions filling our homes — if we had no restraints, what would our everyday look like?

What would an ideal day be like?

How would we work and play?

What would our family times be like? Would we talk, imagine, invent together? How often and how long and where and when would we get together?

What kinds of things might we do alone and together that we have always wanted to do if we only had the opportunity?

What would happen in our times alone? What resources do we need to think and work alone the best?

What would our homes look like? How would we choose to fill them so that each new possession supported maintenance, sustenance or growth of the family?

WHAT IF???????????

What if the entire family went back to school or the entire family earned money for the family or the
    entire family took an extended journey?
What if we filled our home to please the people who lived inside it so that it contained the very
    favorite colors and textures and shapes and light qualities and patterns of each individual in the
    family?
What if we weren't a family, what would be different?
What if we were all 10 years younger and had the same decisions to make?
What if there *were* no every day? What would we imagine it to be? How would time, space, energy
    and other givens be used?

For some of us, imagining starting from zero might help us see the key actions we must take to create a
    satisfying everyday.
For some of us, there may be big questions that must be confronted before we can go anywhere else.
Am I really happy with my situation for myself and my family?
What WOULD I be doing if I weren't doing what I'm doing now?
Where can I start, even in a small way, to get to where I REALLY want to be?

2. WILDMANNING

Another viewpoint to try is to imagine new possibilities for dealing with what is already in the everyday. To be really effective, we must open the floodgates and let all the ideas out — no matter how trivial or wild or impractical they may seem at first. Sometimes the very best of all actions to take will turn out to be trivial or wild or initially impractical. So, for a time at least, we must suspend our critical eye and let our imagination take over.

How big can we think?

How wild can we imagine?

How many possibilities can we dream up?

WHAT IF??????????

We switched the functions for things around and turned the closet into a workroom and the kitchen into a laboratory and a bedroom into a library?

We switched family functions around, too, so that the dishwasher became the social director, and the babysitter reorganized the shelves and the repairer became the inventor and the trash hauler the gardener and never let any one person get stuck with any one role?

We doubled up on the partially wasted times? We used grocery shopping as a time to hunt for colors? We used freeway traveling as a time to practice singing? We used getting-dressed time as a time to plan how to enter the day? We used chore time as a time to imagine big ideas? We used bath time as a storytelling time? We made new kinds of matches between needs and resources so that our special family time happened early in the morning instead of in the evening or we took turns using the same space to be alone to think or we used television watching as a time to investigate the effects of media on ourselves and our families?

We changed the pacing or mood or rhythm of the way we did things and made getting off somewhere times slow and thoughtful and quiet and chore doing times brisk and efficient and after school or after work times bouncy and energetic?

We invented our own kinds of celebrations — like a birthday party of running, jumping, skipping, climbing, tumbling, balancing, and swinging for a child that really loves movement?

Each possibility we imagine can be tried and evaluated until we begin to develop a flexibility of function for everyday things to suit our needs.

3. GETTING DOWN TO BASICS

Another way to visualize taking action is to pare things down to essentials. We can really question the necessity of each object, attitude, dialogue, appointment and possession filling our everyday and work to rid ourselves of any but the most positive and essential. In this way we can clarify our real needs and values, match them more closely to what is an everyday reality and in getting rid of excesses simultaneously create more opportunities for spontaneity and invention.

Do we have the everyday resources we need for:

(1) Alone activities such as:

looking?
listening?
drawing?
making things?
practicing?
wondering?
writing?
collecting favorite things?

inventing surprises?
imagining?
planning?
evaluating?
keeping notes on the day?
investigating?
studying?

(2) Family activities such as:

a picnic?
a family council?
a bake-off?
scientific experiments?
acrobatic tricks?
a puppet show?
building things?
making music?

raising things?
telling stories?
playing games?
sending messages?
dancing?
writing songs?
sharing memories?
making up plays?

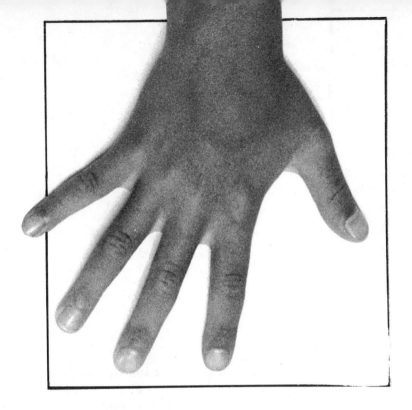

WHAT IF?????????

    I ran errands only once a day?
    I eliminated 90% of my fussiness, complaints, nagging, etc.?
    I repeated the same words as few times as I could stand it?
    I threw out everything I hadn't used in two years?
    I decided we didn't need a living room because we didn't use it enough?
    I organized our house like an efficiency expert?
    I streamlined the way chores were done?

    For some of us it is not more resources that are needed but more carefully selected ones really to make the difference.

4.   CHANGING ME

Another point of view is one which assumes that nothing in our situation or the people around us will change at all. All we can do is to change our own behaviors to make things more like we want them to be. We imagine that routines and rituals and rules and regulations and reponsibilities will be unendingly the same and that we cannot change anyone else's mind or expect them finally to see the light. We, ourselves, are the ONLY agent for change. For example, we can imagine that we will never be able to interest anyone else in keeping the house well-organized or in learning new ways to talk to each other. This means we must see ourselves as the only organizer or inventor of new family dialogues. To use this strategy effectively we cannot secretly hold onto the idea that something will turn up or someone will come around. Even the emergencies and problems that arise will be the same kind we have always had to deal with. Just for a moment we imagine overwhelming sameness and wonder what can we ourselves change to make things more as we want them to be?

We must imagine how we can do something positive even if no one else:
remembers to clean up
listens to anyone else
thinks of new things for the family to do together
thinks past his/her own needs and feelings
contributes his/her efforts to the home's enhancement
does anything unless he/she is told to do so.

WHAT IF??????????

I just let go of bad feelings
I decided never to be bored
I decided never to wait for anything
I decided I didn't have to turn off
I decided I didn't have to get tired
I decided I could do more than I thought I could in a day.
I thought of something new to do the next time I felt like a martyr
I dealt with my anger the way I want my child to deal with his
I wrote my problems like a soap opera, drew them like cartoons, did something to give me the
     perspective of distance
I started each day with a question, a problem, a puzzle to sink my teeth into
I decided to get as interested in the things I don't like as the things I do like
I started by being very quiet and listening to myself
I looked at my child for energy ideas
I used traveling time to let go of where I was and get ready for where I will be
I thought of after work as the most exciting (instead of tiredest) time of the day
I sang a song or did something to put a new rhythm in my head
I practiced changing without skipping a beat
See things I never really noticed
Plan what's happening next
Practice relaxing
Make lists of things that can be accomplished in 5 minutes or so
Read
Invent puzzles in my head
Exercise

Keep going...

KEEP IMAGINING A NEW EVERYDAY !

The whole of everyday must be re-imagined: its character, its flow, its purpose and its heartbeat. We must further imagine how we might maintain and administer, enrich and improve, and create mutually supportive systems every day.

Each new thought I think
Deed I do
Each time I put my hand
To change
Time
Space
Situations
Unfolds
A wider and wider
Pyramid of possibilities
For me
And for my child.

MAINTAINING

IMAGINE WAYS TO MAINTAIN EVERYDAY

The heartbeat of everyday is its maintenance. All of those everyday rituals and routines that keep us fed, clothed, cleaned, and rested are mundane but absolutely essential. We either do each of these personally or instruct and keep tabs on whomever we have delegated to do the chores, preparations, cleaning and upkeep. Maintenance also means maintenance of relationships within the home — the recurring exchanges that are the baseline of our interactions with each other. Maintenance can be suffocating with all its many tiny problems, jobs, decisions and repetitions. Maintenance can be a strain for us whether we ignore it or work too hard at it. But the maintenance of everyday can be a time of renewal, a time to care for our environment and each other, a time to feel once again the stability and strength of the everyday.

BYLAWS FOR EVERYDAY LIVING

We can imagine that we must work out the details of everyday maintenance completely beforehand and submit it to group approval. Nothing must be included that is not absolutely essential to everyday upkeep and necessary to do again and again repeatedly. The laws we write should allow functions to change and should not specify who does what but rather cover the quality of everyday maintenance and its execution. In this way we should draft a document designed to meet our needs, express our values and realize some of our hopes simultaneously.

WHAT IF??????????

We equated cleaning with care or exquisite craftsmanship?
Cooking became a creative everyday activity?
Preparations of all kinds were moments to reflect, not rush?
People in the family made a point to notice and honor each other's homecomings?
We all paused five seconds before answering each other to consider a new and refreshing response?
We didn't expect any one person to be "in charge" of the house?

By-laws for everyday living can be a stabilizing element in the everyday that bridge the gap between what we want the everyday to be and what it must contain.

ON THE GO POLICIES

This time we assume that we will not always be able to work out all the details of an everyday design at once. Most of our time will be spent in getting through the day rather than planning how to make the most of it all. Or, perhaps we find it hard to change everything at once and need to concentrate on changing one thing at a time. Whatever the reasons, sometimes it is best to devise on-the-go policies for everyday living. This means we will generally be responding spontaneously to what occurs every day, but we will be fortified by some prior decisions about what tack to take when certain situations arise. For example, what kinds of things can I imagine doing to handle bad feelings, boredom, emergency, physical problems, unmet expectations and interruptions of plans?

WHAT IF??????????

I decide beforehand how to respond to arguments within the family?
I list for myself behaviors I will not accept from myself or others?
I make myself a suggestion box of things to do when I feel bad or see someone else feeling bad?
I make reminders of things to do when boredom sets in?
I organize the information I might need for various kinds of emergencies and put them where I can get to them fast?
I make a policy always to listen and ask questions before I decide?
I let other people solve their own interaction problems and refuse to get involved?

On-the-go policies force us beforehand to declare boundaries so that we know when to say yes, when to say no and when to change into another direction.

ENRICHING

IMAGINE WAYS TO ENRICH EVERYDAY

We cannot merely make it through a day, we must imagine how a day can be sustaining, renewing, fulfilling and surprising. Everyday should feed our minds with new ideas, stimulate our senses with its sounds and sights and bring us moments of joy, excitement and beauty. We must imagine what it would take everyday to do this.

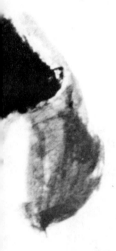

WHAT IF??????????

We displayed mementoes, collections and other favorite objects so we could enjoy them everyday?
We made a tiny museum in a corner of the house to display our best accomplishments of the week?
Before we purchased new objects for the home, we carefully considered the color, texture and other qualities?
We had strict rules about noise and litter pollution inside and outside the home?
Each of us took turns creating a centerpiece or conversation piece for meals?
We took routine trips to the library for "picture books" that made us see things differently?
We selected special music as a background for different everyday routines?
We watched TV like famous critics and discussed what we saw?

For the enrichment of everyday, our imaginations must be given a full and easy reign.

SUPPORTING

IMAGINE
MUTUALLY SUPPORTIVE EVERYDAY SYSTEMS

Everyday should be a place where we support the best in each other and a place where the activities we do together are mutually rewarding.

We want to see each person, even the youngest, contributing what he can to the family as a whole.

Our homes need to be maintained, our resources located and organized, our needs rethought, our endeavors as a team sustained and our flagging everyday energies renewed. Each person can contribute his talents to make home a place that supports and refreshes us.

I'll tell you what I won't
Do
I won't nag
I won't ignore
I won't rush in to pick up your pieces
I will
Give you a chance
Watch you with care
Listen to your errors
Let you know what I like.

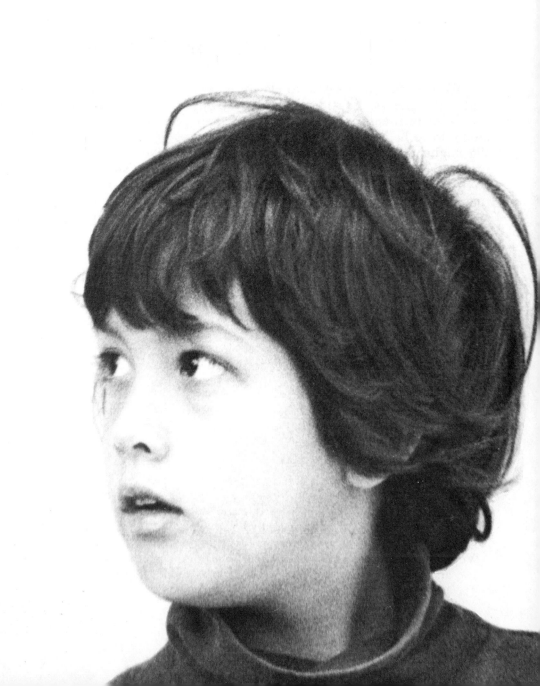

CLARIFYING CHOICES

We may find it of value to clarify what the individuals in our families must choose to do for themselves. To support, especially our children, most effectively we must be able to point out to them the pros and cons of their potential actions, the kinds of things they could do to help themselves grow and the types of decisions they and they alone must make. We might imagine all the kinds of feedback — spoken and unspoken — that we can give others that helps them understand what they're doing and what effects their actions are having on themselves and other people. In essence, we can imagine ourselves as a mirror for our family members and reflect back to them their actions so they can see them more clearly. This is not the same as nagging — the idea is to put responsibility squarely on the individual, where it belongs.

WHAT IF??????????

We told our children one thing we liked about their behavior every single day?

We told our children when "No" really and truly meant "no"?

We told our children what we meant when we asked them to help around the house?

We told our children as many reasons for doing or not doing something as we could think of?

We provided opportunities for our child to learn about other people in other cultures and situations and how they make everyday decisions so our child had more ideas of the consequences of his own decisions?

If we can change
Time and Space
We can change
Ourselves
We can find new ways
To communicate
New words to say
New topics to pursue
We can find new ways
To operate
To invent
To respond
If I can change
Time and space
I can change habits
Too.

WORKING AS A TEAM

For some of us it is almost impossible to imagine making any significant everyday changes without getting the entire family in the act. For all of us, there are times when the power of the group can indeed make much more happen than an individual alone. Using this strategy, we imagine what we might do of value together and how to get everyone working as a team. We must consider how we can delineate for the rest of the family the observations we have made. We can communicate to them the potentials we envision and what the group might do to be effective. We should think through what unique contributions each individual has to make to the group and how to coordinate all efforts.

WHAT IF??????????

We scheduled nights to work together and nights to work all alone?
We took turns having a room all to ourselves to think?
We made a family policy about special family times?
We took turns doing chores to give each other more time?
We made one day a week ''spontaneous day'' and tried to plan for nothing for that day?
We taught each other our tricks for solving problems?
We traded situations for a day?
We tried to respond in the other's world?
We looked at each other with magic ''first time'' glasses? What would we see?
We tried to see how much we could invent in a day?
We made our own code to each other as a warning we were falling into old habits?
We re-ran our arguments a different way each time till we solved them?
We kept thinking of only the positives, not the negatives of each other?

The more we invent together the more we can come to understand both the power and uniqueness of our family and the special hard-to-know-any-other-way qualities of the individual family members. This strategy, if applied, yields surprising by-products of renewed mutual respect and interest in one another.

CREATING POSITIVE DIALOGUES

What shall we say to each other?

Much of our day is taken up with dialogues — verbal exchanges between people. Sometimes our ways of talking to each other have fallen into deadly predictable patterns. We no longer respond to each other with spontaneity and curiosity. We have forgotten how to make something new happen between us. We don't like our relationships to be so rigid but it takes courage and imagination to change them.

But dialogues can be changed; new dialogues can be imagined. We do not have to remain in the same verbal patterns. We can initiate new conversations with each other, and we can respond in new ways to old conversations that are begun.

WHAT IF?????????

We created new kinds of message centers on the refrigerator or in the hall or left each other notes under a pillow or in a drawer?

We made group diaries on the day to compare viewpoints, interests and evaluations?

We tried family councils, family debates, family lecture series, family seminars?

We created a drama night, or music night, or storytelling night to talk to each other in new ways?

We talked without using words?

We drew our feelings? pantomimed our thoughts?

We wrote each other messages?

We wrote each other poems?

We communicated by doing something together? a chore? a game?

We communicated by making something together or learning something together?

We listened or looked or touched the same thing at the same time?

What would we learn about each other?

In the area of dialogues, our children have few positive models to follow. There are few examples of how to talk about ideas together, how really to listen to each other, how to support each other's endeavors and how to say what we really mean to each other. We must create new models ourselves for talking to our children. We must try out verbal and even non-verbal ways of talking about the everything from our most cherished ideals to the most mundane logistics. We want to be able to get accurate information from each other, to have ideas together, to analyze situations together and to evaluate the past together. We want to keep telling each other what positive things we see in each other. We want to stop wasting time in games and old habits and really enjoy our relationships together.

My child will know
There's more to me
Than
"Wait"
"In a minute" and
"Can't you see I'm tired?"
And I will know more of him
Than
"Can I? Can I?"
"Why?" and
"You don't understand!"
Here and now
We will share
"I wonder..."
"Let's try it!"
"I like the way you do things"
Right here and now
We will share
Laughter
Ideas
Work
And curiosities.

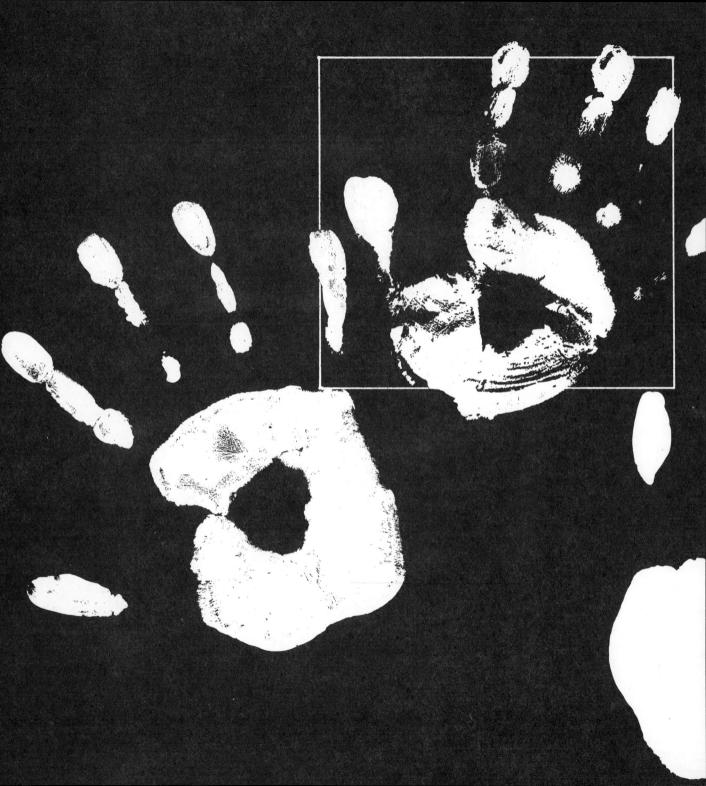

INVENT

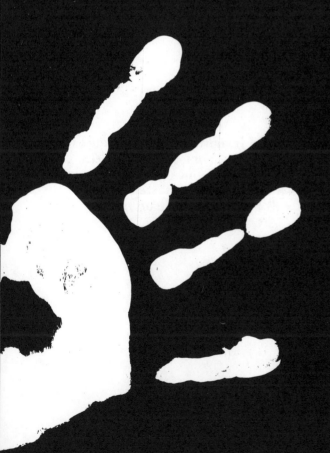

I'm going to build a day
For you
(And me)
It will be strong and sturdy
Yet
Flexible
Filled with problems but also
Flooded with solutions
It will be steady
Yet ever changing
Demanding
Yet yielding
A day to maintain
Sustain
Clarify
And renew
(Me and
You)

Now that we have inventoried the whole of everyday and imagined ways to change it better to suit ourselves and our families, we are prepared to select from our many ideas, give them tangible form and try them out. Everyday will not be invented once but continuously as we unendingly improve everyday and change it to keep up with us. Each step in the process is critical — this one no less so. All our efforts will be in vain if we do not understand the importance of creating everyday form.

CREATING FORM

Forms capture meaning in the everyday. Forms are tangible expressions of ideas.

Forms turn decisions into realities, reinforce new habits and support solutions to problems. There are forms of work, play, exploration and experimentation. There are forms in which to collect new information, forms that give us feedback; even forms in which to think new thoughts.

Forms are shaped by thoughts, hands, voices, bodies. Forms are made of words, wood, numbers, stone, paint. When we create dialogues, interactions, social exchanges, routines, rituals, and celebrations, we create forms that express meaning.

Forms are invented, created, modeled, designed, structured, built and patterned to symbolize, communicate, express and represent an identity, a meaning, a knowledge, a value. We create form continuously although the form may have been invented many times before.

What forms can we create that will promote growth and satisfaction for ourselves and our children? We can create situations that make it easy for everyone to get involved. We can arrange time, space and materials so that they allow us to work alone and together. We can keep re-arranging things until our children have the resources that work for them. We can provide opportunities to communicate with our children about their work and ideas. We can initiate family projects and organize ways to get all of us working and contributing to the maintenance and enhancement of our home. We can structure things so that everyone gets a chance to share his needs and suggestions with everyone else.

When we give tangible form to our ideas; when we create words, gestures, events — we are not only expressing ideas to our child, our family, our world — but are giving ourselves perspective toward ongoing experience. A form, once produced, becomes a part of the texture of experience, a resource of new information. A form reminds us of what has passed and suggests changes for the future.

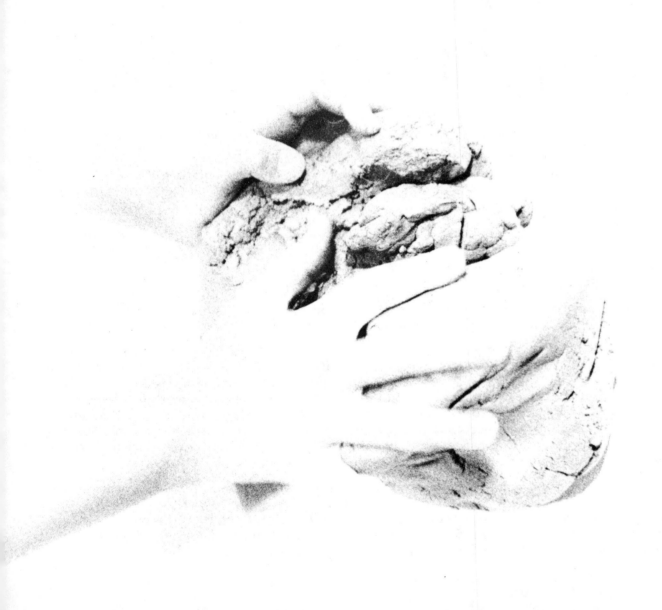

Inventors work with the givens.
They get to know their material,
Understand how it responds,
Know what it can and can't do.
When they invent, they don't complain
about their givens.
(A brick can't change its shape.)
They make the most exciting use of
what they have.
The everyday inventor has givens, too.
Time
Space
Energy
Some are pretty resistant.
(As unchangeabler as a brick?)

INVENTING
EVERYDAY FORMS

(1) New interactions with each other that allow mutual growth and change.

    (a)   Social Forms

        We must invent ways to be together and enjoy each other. For example, instead of sitting passively watching TV, each of us insulated from the other, we must invent ways to share our experiences, hopes, talents and interests. This includes simple inventions, like five minutes to share our day and more elaborate inventions such as birthday celebrations.

    (b)   Communication Forms

        We must invent new ways to talk to each other. We must be able to create ways to get our messages to others in verbal and non-verbal ways. We must invent small ways to communicate things such as logistics and big ways to communicate important ideas and values.

(2) New ways to maintain our everyday living
We must invent structures that help us to organize and maintain the givens of everyday living: eating, cleaning, preparing, traveling, and so on. To do so, we must create many smaller inventions: schedules and procedures to improve efficiency; surprises, games and atmospheres that eliminate drudgery and boredom; functional roles that can be changed so everyone in the family learns to shape a day in different ways.

(3) Environments that promote everyday creativity
We must invent, especially for our children, situations in which they can explore, create and experiment on their own terms. We must make time and space for them so that they can come to know themselves, their abilities and interests; be able to express their feelings and represent their ideas in form; and develop an understanding of how they uniquely invent.

(4) Celebrations of values
There are times we want to emphasize and make special, to give size and scope. We must invent these times of celebration as a means to redefine comprehensively what we value in each other and our environment, why we are a family and what is most meaningful to us. These big events capture and make tangible the big ideas we wish to keep in the forefront. They give us a point of reference with which to compare our everyday actions and events. They help us to keep our perspective about what our tiny everyday actions are totalling.

The benefits of conscious, fresh invention are enormous. Invention gives our everyday surprise, curiosity, joy. Invention is somewhere between work and play. It takes energy, consistency and endurance. And when we stretch limitations to create something new, we gain a new sense of self.

What shall we say
To each other
If we take
The space and time?
Could we change
The way
We always talk
Could we share
A concern
A job
An idea?

Conversation starters:

What's the problem?
What do you want to happen?
Give me the straight facts.
What are your reasons for your actions?
Whoa! I didn't mean to say that. Let me try again.
What would you like to get out of all this?
I have an idea.
I'm going to try something new just to see if it will help.
We goofed but will keep trying. Right?
If you really want my attention, say "Mommy" in a strong, unwhiny voice.
This is what I want.
I'll tell you how I was looking at it. You tell me how you were looking at it.
Let's get un-mad before we talk.
I want to tell you how I feel when you do that.
What are the limits?

To create new dialogues, we need to keep working at it. It may take several tries at what kinds of dialogues are most beneficial and many hours of practicing responding in a new way really to get the long-range power more flexible dialogues can bring.

We need room to move
So let's push back the tables
We need to work
So let's pull up a chair
We need to be alone so
Let's put a wall between us
We need to be together
So let's share.

I have to say it
To myself
Or I lose it
I have to remember
Why I'm doing things
Or I forget
I have to remind me
What's important
Or it slips away.

Say it big
If you want me to hear
What's important
Do it big
If you want to know
The right actions
Make it big
So I can see it
And remember
What it means.

I think I see
What you wanted me
To see and
Now know what you
Hoped I'd believe
You made a special
Day
An event
To make it real
To make it big
You showed me
Something valuable
To you
And I think I see
What you see
I think I see it
Too.

Without variation, a new design for everyday maintenance can become just as deadly repetitious as the old one. We need to vary what we do every day so we keep a fresh viewpoint toward what is happening and continue changing things to suit our needs.

WHAT DO WE NEED TO VARY?

Routines	People chores	Work and play
Getting ready	Space usage	Speed
Cleaning up	Object functions	Mood
Traveling	Eating	Size
Rituals	Conversing	Attitude

We don't have to turn off,
Feel bad,
Act bored,
Do we?
We can choose
To get interested,
Stay curious
Can't we?
There isn't a rule,
Is there?
I don't have to
Give up,
Do I?

My everyday
Must fit the needs
Of me and mine
Must yield us
Possibilities
For being and becoming
My design of everyday
Must build in time for
Reflection
And redefinition
Of my day
And of the design
Itself.

REFLECT

In my mind
I re-arrange the furniture
Turn an idea over
A thought around
I imagine a completely new design
Invent a wildly different floor plan
Bring in new information
Eliminate
Re-order
Re-define
In the end I may put it back
As it was
But this time
I remember why.

After we have acted to make real our hopes and wishes for our family, we must look back on all we have done and evaluate what happened. We must examine our actions and ask ourselves if they have helped us to create more closely an everyday that meets the needs of our family as a group and as individuals.

Reflective time is essential because it puts distance between ourselves and our actions and allows us to determine whether or not what we've done has been effective.

WHAT HAPPENED?
WHAT HAPPENED?
WHAT HAPPENED?
WHAT HAPPENED?

DID IT HELP?
DID IT HELP?
DID IT HELP?
DID IT HELP?

WHAT HAPPENED??????????

Did the forms we created support everyday maintenance?
Did the forms we created enrich the whole of everyday?
Did the forms we created improve our systems of mutual endeavor and communication?
Did we create forms to make better use of time, space, energy and so on?

Do the forms created reflect our everyday values?
Do they fulfill everyday needs?
Do they meet everyday hopes?

Do the forms of everyday allow for more responsiveness, initiation, diversity, sharing, support,
    flexibility, problem-solving, resourcefulness and creativity?
If our forms are not doing what we wish them to, what might we create that would?

I begin to see
How a day is adding up
What I can make of a day
What a day can make of me
I begin to see
That I have a choice
That I can take a hand
In the design of my everyday
I begin to see
How I can belong
To me.

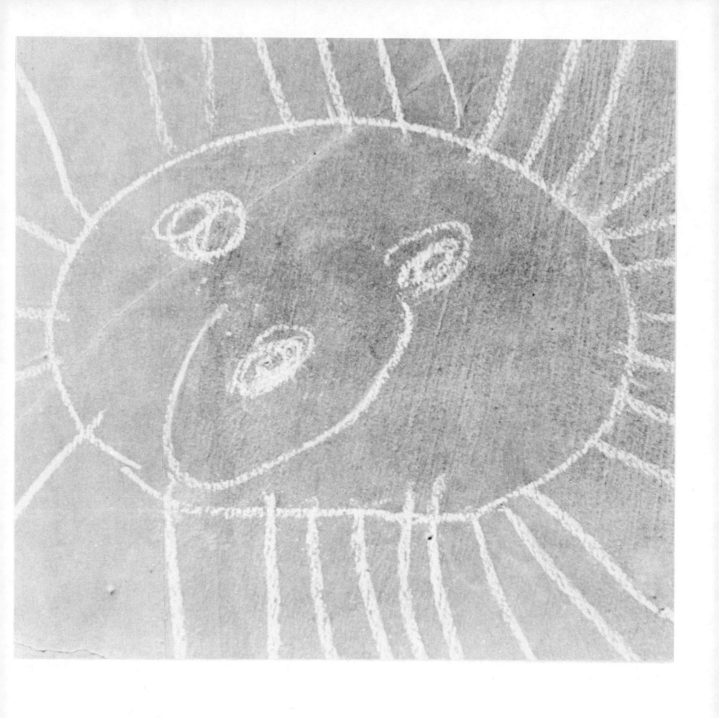

PART TWO
CREATE

A CHILD'S EVERYDAY

Not only can the everyday be re-created, it can be custom-designed to promote the growth of our children. The opportunity some of us had while growing up to explore our world, practice new behaviors, discover our own special identities — can be created by us in the present for our children. The everyday needs more than shaping — it must be shaped into a context that supports and develops a child's unique potential. We parents are best qualified to do this because we know most about our child and his/her world.

This half of the book is best used by the concerned adult to help the child. Eventually the child her/himself will become more able to reflect on his/her own special qualities and help create an environment to nurture those qualities, too.

Two courses of action are suggested:

IMPROVE — review the everyday and restructure it to provide opportunities for individual growth.

INDIVIDUALIZE—assess the uniqueness of your child and create specific forms to support that individuality and strengthen its development.

IMPROVE

The everyday structure so far created must
be refined in order to provide opportunities
for our child to locate and develop his/her
potential. In this context we may re-analyze
everyday resources and restructure them to
allow the child to work and play independently
and creatively and to initiate and contribute his/her
creative talents to the family as a whole.

This time as we inventory the everyday, we do more than list what is there: we look
for the best qualities in what is there. These will be the resources we use to create custom-
designed opportunities for our child to create.

EVERYDAY RESOURCES TO BE USED BY MY CHILD:

Look for resources which can be used in the process of invention:
raw materials, idea sources, contents, supportive elements.

TIMES

Morning
Afternoon
Evening
Five minutes
One hour
A day
A week
Summer
School year

ROUTINES

Preparing
Going and coming
Cleaning
Eating
Working
Playing

PEOPLE

Family
Friends
Acquaintances
Experts
Fictional and real
Relatives

SPACES

Inside
Outside
Different rooms
Ceiling
Floor
Walls
Windows
Doors
Trees

MATERIALS

Natural
Re-cycled
Multi-use
Re-usable

QUALITIES

Light and shadow
Shapes
Color
Textures
Motion
Rhythm
Sounds

I'm going to stop
Playing fair
I'm going to stop
Playing at all
I'm going to give
You
What I can
and what you
Would really like
Not anything
And everything
Anyone
Else has.

ANALYZE EVERYDAY RESOURCES

time

Time is an everyday resource. No matter how structured and crowded a day there are always those times when we wait for something, get bored, turn off or can't find anything to do. There are also times spent traveling or dressing or doing simple chores that can also be utilized for thinking, for planning, for imagining, for wondering alone. We can improve the times we spend with our children. We can use those times to be more responsive, to listen to what our child really needs, to play and work together. There are other times our child needs to be alone, to try things out, to initiate projects, to experiment, explore and invent. We can give our children time to come to know themselves and their possibilities.

HOW MANY, HOW MUCH, HOW OFTEN, HOW BIG?

What times do I want for us everyday?
How can they fit in?
  — alone time for each of us? time for thinking, reflecting, reading, playing, working?
  — time to share with my child — a curiosity, an experiment, a surprise?
  — time for all of us to think together, talk together?

space

Space is an everyday resource. Space may be at a premium and strictly cut up, but there are always spaces that never get used, outdoor as well as indoor spaces, spaces that can serve more than one purpose, spaces that can be traded or reserved, spaces where furniture can be re-arranged. There are other overlooked spaces such as cars, windows, closets, under tables and even walls that might serve our needs. Mainly we need spaces to be together and spaces to be alone. The nice thing about space is we can try lots of possibilities, and if we don't like any of them, we can put things back as they were. Spaces can be changed to suit people (and ought to be, instead of the other way around).

HOW MANY, HOW MUCH, HOW OFTEN, HOW BIG?

Are the spaces we have the ones we need for our everyday?
— spaces for alone, quiet thoughts
— spaces for action and movement
— spaces for experimenting, working with materials
— spaces for sharing and discussing

energy

Energy is an everyday resource. Energy isn't created or destroyed. It's always there, waiting to be transformed from one thing to another. Energy is a process, always in motion. It can be transferred among people, things, ideas — a person making an idea happen, an idea making an event happen.

There are hidden pockets of energy in the fabric of everyday — energy in emotions, group consensus, unexpected changes, times of transition, children, chores.

Overlooked sources of energy can be called on and utilized. We can help our children understand their tremendous questions and curiosity, can transform work, play ideas.

HOW MANY, HOW MUCH, HOW OFTEN, HOW BIG?

What do we need energy for every day?
- — energy for the maintenance jobs of every day
- — energy for asking questions, imagining, trying out new ideas
- — energy for each other, for supporting a group plan or project, for listening and discussing, for sharing ideas and information

people

People can be one of the best everyday resources available to a child. Older people have skills and memories to share. Other children can participate in our child's ideas. People are a terrific source of information whether our child talks to them, interacts with them in other ways or simply watches and listens to them. We parents are also a people resource and can take on many functions: audience, partner, evaluator, teacher and so on.

HOW MANY, HOW MUCH, HOW OFTEN, HOW BIG?

What people will best stimulate my child's work and imagination? How much time does he need with people? How much time alone?

I find a little silence
In the day
To spend alone
In the quiet
I catch the day and see
What I can make of it.
I plumb my imagination
To make more of what I have
To give my child.
I want our times together
To be joyful and relaxed,
Spontaneous
And alive.

RESTRUCTURE RESOURCES

Notice_!

Starting Monday from 4:00-5:00 we will all invent, play or experiment alone —

No TV, No friends

We'll share what we did at dinner on Friday.

Thanks—

Mom

More of the structures of everyday can be open-ended so that the child has an opportunity to contribute his/her talents and viewpoint and so come to understand them better. In addition, the everyday must include unstructured times during the day in which the child operates alone and is encouraged to play, dream, invent, experiment, explore, collect, imagine, test, practice and create. Only through having to structure his own entertainment and activities at recurrent times during the everyday will the child be able to locate and develop his unique potential.

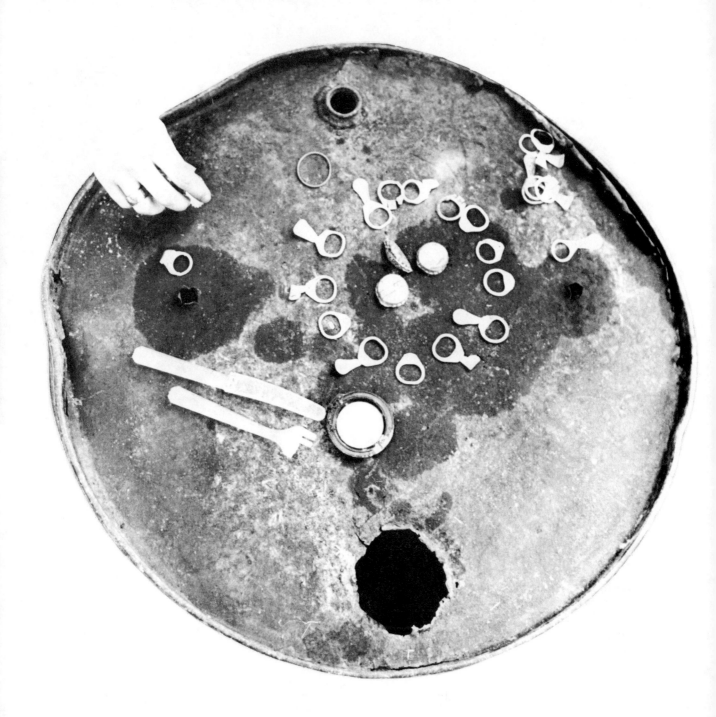

RESTRUCTURE EVERYDAY TO ALLOW A CHILD TO LEARN ABOUT HIMSELF

Provide him with times he must structure by himself. Turn off TV, extracurricular activities and pressures from friends for a time.

Let him use a space to be alone and work, to arrange and organize in his own way.

RESTRUCTURE RESOURCES SO THAT A CHILD HAS A CHANCE TO INITIATE WITHIN THE FAMILY

It is important, but not sufficient, that a child be able to operate independently and also contribute to the family. She/he also must be able periodically to structure what the family does and to feel the family support what he tries. This means he should be given some opportunity to structure how chores will be done or plan and cook a meal for the family or create an entertainment for the family or involve the family in one of his projects. These opportunities will give him more confidence and feedback on his creative endeavors.

Allow and encourage:
    play
    invention
    experimentation
    investigation
    questioning
    daydreaming
    fooling around with possibilities
    practice of new behaviors
    initiation within the family
    presentation of own ideas

My policies for getting the most
From a day
Are to go fast
On the "have tos"
Go easy on the "shoulds"
"Musts" and "only one ways"
Go slow on the pretty things
(Especially if they're hidden)
Go creative on the routines
Go deep and busy on the alone times
Go happy and surprising on the
"Togethers"
And when you get through
Go back over it all.

INDIVIDUALIZE

The final step in the process of refinement is to individualize everyday according to your individual child. Although children share many things in common, each is unique and special. Each child has a way of looking at his world, imagining possibilities, thinking about ideas, working and operating that is unique. His creativity is unique and demands unique everyday resources in order to develop. This means not just providing opportunities to invent — but the specific kinds of opportunities that suit her/him best. This means not just providing her/him a space and materials for work and play but the exact ones she/he needs. This means not just participating in his/her ideas but in the special way that will help him/her the most.

To make this final step we must first assess, in our own estimation, our child's individual qualities and then both tangibly support them and customize the everyday to promote them.

To develop creatively, a child must gain a sense of what about himself is special and must learn that it is most satisfying to work on his own terms and create that which will benefit himself and other people.

HOW CAN I SEE WHAT'S SPECIAL IN MY CHILD?

WHAT IF??????????

I pretend I'm seeing him/her for the first time?
I look beyond my child's personality?
     if she/he is loud — what kind of loud?
     if she/he is active — what kind of active?
I watch my child when she/he doesn't know I'm looking?
I get my child to take me on a tour of a place she/he likes and I notice what she/he notices?
I play a variety of games with my child to discover how she/he likes to play?
I bring home a ''picture book'' to look at together and notice what she/he likes?
I take my child to a very new and different environment and observe what she/he says and notices?
I follow my child through his/her day and take notes like a reporter?
I ask my child to make imaginary choices (would you rather live in a jungle or in the Arctic?) to see
     how his/her imagination works?

You renew
Me
When I really look at you
Really respond
You renew me
When I forget all else
But the amazing
Unfolding of
You
I am renewed

ASSESS YOUR CHILD'S INDIVIDUALITY

(1) What are the qualities of your child that make him/her unique?
(2) What qualities does he/she seem especially to prefer?
(3) What are his/her self-initiated activities?
(4) What is your child's style of thinking, learning and working?

1. UNIQUE QUALITIES OF A CHILD

How does my child sound? What is the quality of voice? the speed of conversation? the strength or softness?

How does my child move? What is the quality of my child's walk, way of standing, sitting, moving, pausing? How often does my child move and with what strength and size and intent?

What is the rhythm of my child? busy, slow and steady, intense, bounding, still, surprising, forthright? What kind of pace does he/she have?

How does my child use face and eyes? What do they typically communicate? What are my child's expressions to another?

How does my child present a public face? How does it differ from the private face I know! How do other people respond to my child?

What kinds of roles and functions does my child prefer to take on? leader? supporter? listener? performer? director? interviewer? conformist? devil's advocate?

What is my child's sense of humor?

What are his joys?

What questions does he ask again and again?

What make his viewpoint different from anyone else's?

Impulses have two faces.
The bully in you would make a fine director.
The worrier you are has a wonderfully fluent imagination.
The stubborn side is also the side that asks questions.
Even the nag is the one that cares enough to perfect.

2. QUALITIES A CHILD LIKES

What catches her eye?
  movement
  textures
  colors
  interesting shapes
  strong pattern

What holds his attention?
  sound
  strong rhythm
  people
  environments
  books

What does she love to surround herself with?
  people
  animals
  space
  sound
  things to manipulate

What qualities do his favorite toys and games have?
  big movement
  a certain procedure
  structural components
  strong sound qualities
  special color or textural qualities

What does he collect, naturally? What qualities do they have?
  bugs
  magazines
  broken machines
  ribbons
  hats
  records
  rocks

What kinds of things does my child like to play with? experiment with, invent with?

What kinds of things is my child most likely to notice, comment on, pick up, examine, ask about or save?

What are the qualities of the things my child likes best?
  Are they colorful? What kinds of colors are they? Bright? dull? shiny? soft? dark?
  How do they look or feel to the touch? Are they smooth? nubby? rusty? fuzzy? hard?
    wooden? malleable?
  Do they have definite shapes? Are they extremely simple in contour? Are they intricate?
    Do they have structural parts or possibilities?
  Do they move? Is there a mechanical or natural rhythm to their movement? Is the
    movement smooth, humorous, fast, floating?
  Do they make sounds? What kinds of sound qualities do they produce? ringing? rasping?
    thudding? whirring? whistling? Is there a definite rhythm to the sound they produce?

Are they two-dimensional or three-dimensional? Are they stacked? patterned? put in an order? grouped together?

Do they have a definite linear quality? Are they gently curving? severely angular? strongly directional? repetitive?

What are the spatial qualities that my child notices? the light quality? the structure of the space? the size? the potential for movement in the space?

Which spaces and places does she prefer? kitchen? bedroom? living room? porch? front yard? back yard? school yard? store?

What kinds of interactions does my child like? quiet? rough? direct? dramatic? straight?

What does he spend time really watching or listening to or otherwise soaking up? people interactions? music? chores? patterns? animals? books? how things work?

To get MORE information about what your child likes, try this JUNK BOX GAME:

(1) Give your child a box with a wide assortment of junk, such as:

paper clips	rubber bands
jar tops	buttons
bottle tops	sticks
scarves	straws
rubber ball	tin foil
tin cans	cotton balls
blocks	socks
yarn	paper
crayolas	pens
sponge	

(2) Quietly watch what she/he does with it:

build things	arrange things
take things apart	animate things
stack things	talk to you
talk to self	make a gift
make a decoration	make noises
fit things together	put things in categories

(3) Notate the qualities of the objects used and the things made with the objects.

(4) List all the things you noticed.

this is charlie
hideout.

I *like to think*
In my room alone

I *like to dream*
In a tree

I *like to invent on*
The kitchen table

In the backyard
I *like to run free*

I *like to ponder*
On the living room couch

In the big chair with you
I *read*

I *like to watch things*
Outside my window

Each place in my home
Is a special place
That fits the life
I *lead.*

3. ACTIVITIES A CHILD LIKES

What does he do repeatedly, just for the joy of doing?
   practicing sounds or rhythms
   moving — dancing, running
   watching people
   building
   drawing

What do I see my child spending a lot of time doing?
   making things
   asking questions
   staring at things
   looking at people and how they behave
   thinking out loud
   collecting things
   drawing
   imitating people and animals
   running and jumping
   making up stories
   directing other people
   making jokes
   practicing skills

What does my child choose to do with people?
  play games
  play make believe
  explore and investigate things
  talk
  Who does my child spend time with?

Where does my child like to expend the most energy?
  concentrate the hardest
  devote the most attention

Does my child read, play with toys, climb, watch TV, daydream, sing, experiment, play
  with animals or what? Is time spent on personal projects or on doing homework or
  other jobs?

What does he like to invent?
  drawings
  constructions
  drama
  locations
  machines
  toys
  games
  social events

What does my child like to do with space?
  invent a hideout under a table
  turn a closet into work space
  pretend the living is really a hospital or library or school

How many ways does my child know to try to get what he wants from people?
  by talking loud to get their attention
  by coming straight out and asking
  by teasing in a friendly way
  by changing his tone of voice
  by offering something in exchange

How does my child like to move through space?
   by running and skipping
   by wandering or floating
   Does my child like to sit quietly in a space or shape it up?

With whom does my child like to interact?
   people
   animals
   adults
   peers
   babies
   different kinds of people

Does my child like to interact with large numbers of people at once
   or one at a time or in small groups or what?

How does my child talk to other people? What is talked about?
   ideas
   work
   memories
   plans
   things in the here and now
   events
   people
   things

What projects and social forms does my child initiate with other people?
   picnics
   discussions
   a garden
   a puppet show
   things to make together
   a sing-along

How does my child talk to himself? How much? What does my child say?
   sing songs about daily events
   direct thinking activities
   make up stories about what is happening

The picture I have of me
Is too small
Too bad
Too good
Not quite right
The picture that fits me best
Keeps changing
Keeps moving
Keeps growing
Because I do.

4. A CHILD'S STYLE

What are my child's preferred procedures for working, playing, solving problems, entering new situations, inventing?

How does he/she go about getting a job done?

Does he/she work methodically to take on the whole world? try someone else's way to work first?

How does my child like to organize materials?

How does my child like to organize space? Is it preferred empty so there's lots of room to move? filled with carefully placed objects and materials? crammed and crowded with the project of the moment?

How long does my child spend with any one activity? How often does my child like to switch activities?

How does my child change spaces? quickly? slowly? repeatedly? How long does my child like to operate in a single space before changing?

How does my child represent his ideas the most often? drawing? building? making up stories? acting out plays?

When does my child work the hardest? the fastest? the most accurately?

How does my child solve problems? Which ones are hard for her/him? Which are easy? Which are chronic?

How does my child remember best? What does he/she remember well?

When do things click for my child? When does he/she suddenly go "Aha!"?

WHEN MY
MIND is
WORKING
IT goes like this.
this movement :it
goes by itself

Knowing all the special
Qualities of you
Your humor
Your concern
Your wonderings
Your abilities
I want to help make them
Visible
Everyday
I want to make you the time
Space and resources
To point out all the opportunities
That exist
For you
To be the kind of you
You really are
Everyday.

Support your child's individuality

We parents can foster the qualities we see in our child in two ways: (1) by taking time to interact with our children in the ways they need us most, and (2) by consistently celebrating and honoring the specialness we see in our child.

Once again, exercise your own creativity.

Realize you are in a position to know more about and do more for your child than might anyone else.

Don't just make the opportunity; help your child take advantage of that opportunity.

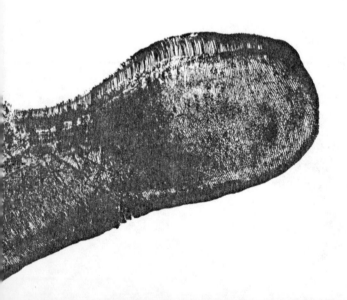

(1) Be the kind of audience he/she needs.
   Does he/she need someone simply to listen to his/her ideas?
   Does he/she need someone to watch him/her perform?
   Does he/she need positive feedback?
   Does he/she need someone to point to qualities in his/her work they especially like?

(2) Participate in the way he/she particularly needs.
   Does he/she need a fellow experimenter?
   Does he/she need a director? an actor?
   Does he/she need someone to accompany him/her on new adventures?
   Does he/she need a temporary assistant?
   Does he/she need an expert to teach him/her or demonstrate?
   Does he/she need someone to trade roles temporarily?

(3) Invent interactions that will support what he/she needs.
   Does he/she need to play little word games?
   Does he/she need to "jam" with music?
   Does he/she need to be read to?
   Does he/she need to take something apart?

What do you need to do with your child?

talk?

listen?

imagine?

collect things?

experiment?

work?

play?

exercise?

invent?

build?

cook?

sew?

draw?   write?

act?   read?

paste?   pretend?

cut out?   practice?

sing?   remember?

dance?   laugh?

I don't know
What
You said
But I remember
How
You said it
I don't hear a
Word
I hear a
Tone
I can't recall
If what
You said
Was important
But I sure do remember
What
You did.

Celebrate

A child learns to value that which is given time, attention and emphasis. A child's special qualities, and the promotion of the growth of those qualities, must be celebrated in great and small ways for her/him to believe in them, too.

How can we make visible what we appreciate in a child?

How can we let him/her know that he/she is different from anyone else?

Dear Cory — The whole family
really enjoyed the sound
and light show you
gave for us last
night! How about
an encore?
Lov

WHAT DO YOU NEED TO CELEBRATE IN YOUR CHILD?

an idea?

a viewpoint?

a sense of humor?

an invention?

a thought?

a memory?

a way of working?

a curiosity?

a strength?

a function or role?

an attitude?

When you talk to me
About what you're doing
And why
Talk to me
About what you want
And how you're working on it
When you talk to me
I hear the answer
Of how to talk
To myself.

Let me be your mirror
As you are mine
Let me reflect
The best parts of you
So you can see
Yourself
As a thinker and
Changer
Filled with ideas
Solutions and
Surprises
Let me be your mirror
Reflecting the very best
Of us both.

Individualized materials and spaces

Last, but not least, we can provide our child with right materials and environment in which to invent, create and experiment. These should be specifically matched to the qualities and preferences we observed in our child. The materials should be those that fit his/her ideas best. The spaces should be those that allow for his/her kind of organization, procedures and aesthetics.

MATERIALS

If we remember back to the materials we observed our child loving the most, then we know which materials to provide him. They must be materials that suit his special way of thinking and working although they can be re-cycled items, still useful throwaways, scrounged materials or bought things. The important thing is to match the materials to the qualities the child loves best: the kinds of colors, textures, shapes, motion, patterns, rhythms, light, sound, lines and spaces that are the most satisfying.

If a child likes:	Try giving him or her:
color	paint, markers, food coloring, colored cellophane, colored paper scraps, bright felt
shapes	mud, clay, dough, scissors and paper materials for stuffed animals
lines	Japanese brush and ink, wire, scraps, yarn, string, thread, pencil and ruler
textures	rusty metal, chalk, fabric, scraps, cotton, straw, package stuffing

space	boxes of all sizes, paper and tape, magazine cutouts (pages are also spaces)
rhythm	patterns and designs of all kinds, costumes and props to make up plays, a huge amount of similar small objects
movement	space to move in, big things to whirl and twirl and flip balls, cylinders of all sizes, rope and things for swings
light	mirrors, tinfoil, glitter, sequins, sparkles
sound	things to bang, blow, pluck, music to hear, sounds to sing, things to rustle, scrape, whirl

Also think of stories the child would like to hear, memories to tell, people to talk to, natural objects to explore, books to read or use as resources, and even: animals, electronic things like radios, tape recorder, typewriters, and cameras, tools such as saws and hammers, and especially everyday junk like bottle caps, package wrappings, junk mail, used containers, scraps from other projects, and even dry food and water.

The best gifts I ever got
Were gifts that needed
Me
Materials to ply
Containers to fill
Bits and pieces to enlarge
With my imagination.

SPACES

Everyone needs an alone space, however small, to call his or her own. Given time to explore personal possibilities, a child needs a space in which to do so. A child needs a space to collect and order ideas, to give them expression and try them out. A child needs a space to fit his or her own unique working pattern. A child needs the opportunity to try out and compare many spaces until a space is designated that really fits the child and supports thinking and working alone.

WHAT KINDS OF SPACES DOES HE/SHE NEED? LIKE?

small? large?

open? closed?

bright? dark?

stark? cluttered?

noisy? silent?

isolated? near people?

inside? outside?

high? low?

stable? portable?

Thanks for letting me experiment
For letting me try things out
There may be a right way
There may be a wrong way
But your're helping me find
My way
Instead.

REFLECT
AGAIN

What happened?

How can I evaluate what happened?
What helped the most?

Now how is my child filling time? Does my child have the kinds of times he needs and in the right proportions?

Am I making more use of the time I have with my child? Do I need more time?

Is my child more able to invent spaces to meet her or his needs? Alone spaces? Group spaces?

Is my child using space more imaginatively?

Is my child seeking out the kinds of materials he or she needs for invention? experimentation?

Is my child making better use of materials that are readily available within the home?

Is my child doing fewer passive things like watching TV?

Is my child more responsive? More initiating? Showing an increased range of interests?

Does my child get busy faster? finish jobs faster? stay interested in investigations longer?

Is my child more positive toward other people?

Is my child taking on a larger variety of roles?

Is my child creating his own kind of social forms?

Do I hear new kinds of dialogues coming from my child?

After we determine which pieces are and are not supporting what we want to happen, we must re-look at everyday in a more holistic fashion. The results of our evaluation can be used to create a design for everyday that integrates the best of what we have learned to do.

I am limited less by
Chance and
Nature
Than by my own vision of me.

Parents are the key to the development of a child's creative potential. Everyday is the context in which this development takes place.

When we parents inventory our everyday, imagine what it might be, re-invent it, improve it and individualize it for our child, we make a difference. We create the best possible environment in which our child can learn and grow. We tangibly model for him the process of creative work. We pass on to him a tradition of re-shaping the world to promote the best in all of us.

Everyday is all we have to give our children.